## Mind Webs

# LIGHT AND SOUND

Anna Claybourne

Illustrated by Chrissy Barnard

First published in Great Britain in 2015 by Wayland

Dewey number: 534-dc23
ISBN: 978 0 7502 8959 7
Library Ebook ISBN: 978 0 7502 8790 6
10 9 8 7 6 5 4 3 2 1

The rights of Anna Claybourne to be identified as the Author and Chrissy Barnard
to be identified as the Illustrator of this Work have been asserted by them
in accordance with the Copyright, Designs and Patents Act, 1988.

Series editor: Victoria Brooker
Series designer: Lisa Peacock

A CIP catalogue record for this book is available
from the British Library.

Wayland is an imprint of Hachette Children's Group
Part of Hodder & Stoughton
Carmelite House
50 Victoria Embankment
London EC4Y 0DZ

Printed in China

An Hachette UK Company
www.hachette.co.uk
www.hachettechildrens.co.uk

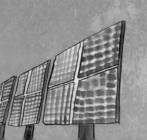

# Contents

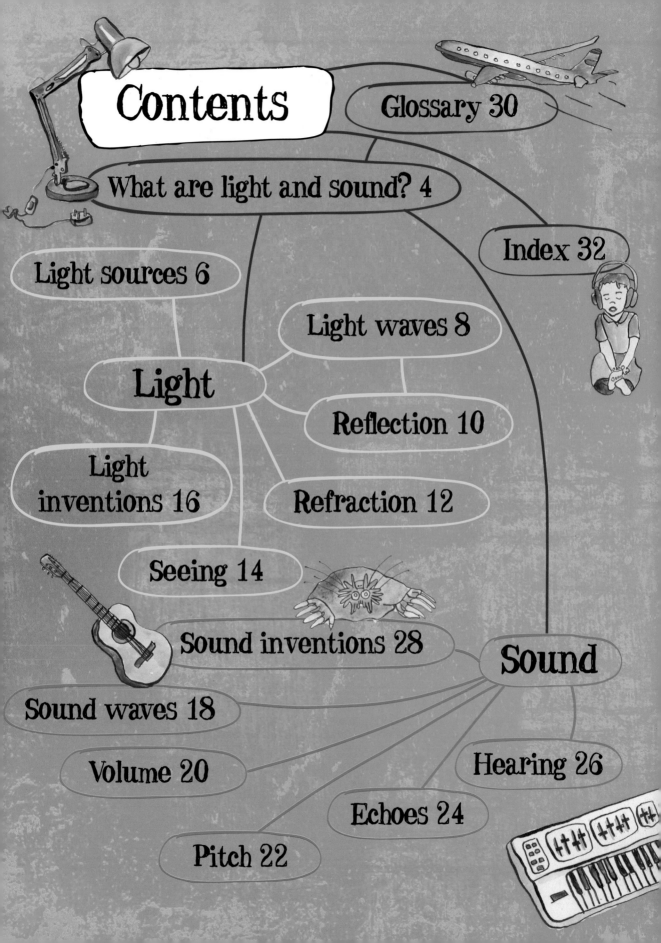

# What are light and sound?

Light and sound are both forms of energy. Energy means the power to do work or make things happen. Whenever anything moves, heats up, changes, grows or gets switched on, some kind of energy is being used. When things glow or shine, it's light energy; when they make a noise, it's sound energy.

Light and sound both spread out from a source, and travel in the form of energy waves. For example, a lit candle is a source of light, and a switched-on radio is a source of sound.

## Using light and sound

Our eyes and ears are constantly sensing patterns of light and sound energy. They tell us a lot about the things around us – and sometimes about things that are far, far away, like stars in the night sky.

Many other living things detect light and sound, too. Most animals can see and hear, and plants rely on light energy to live and grow.

We have discovered how to record light and sound, so that we can play back songs, look at photos, or enjoy films and TV shows with moving images, speech, music and sound effects. We have also developed many other types of light and sound technology, from basic torches and drums to electronic music and optical fibres.

# What is a mind web?

In this book, all the facts you need to know about light and sound are arranged into mind webs. A mind web is a way of laying out information about a topic on a single page. The topic title goes in the middle, with all the important facts and words arranged around it. There are lines to link things together, and little pictures to help you remember things.

Mind webs are very useful for helping you think, learn and sort out ideas. They let you see a topic all at once, showing how all the parts are linked together. Because the mind web looks like a picture, your brain may also find it easier to remember. Mind webs can also be called mind maps, spidergrams or spider graphs. This mini mind web shows the main topics to do with light.

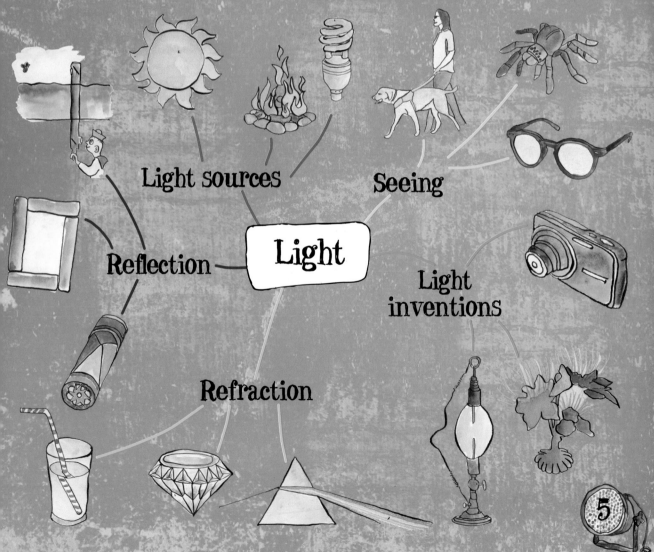

Light sources

Seeing

Reflection

**Light**

Light inventions

Refraction

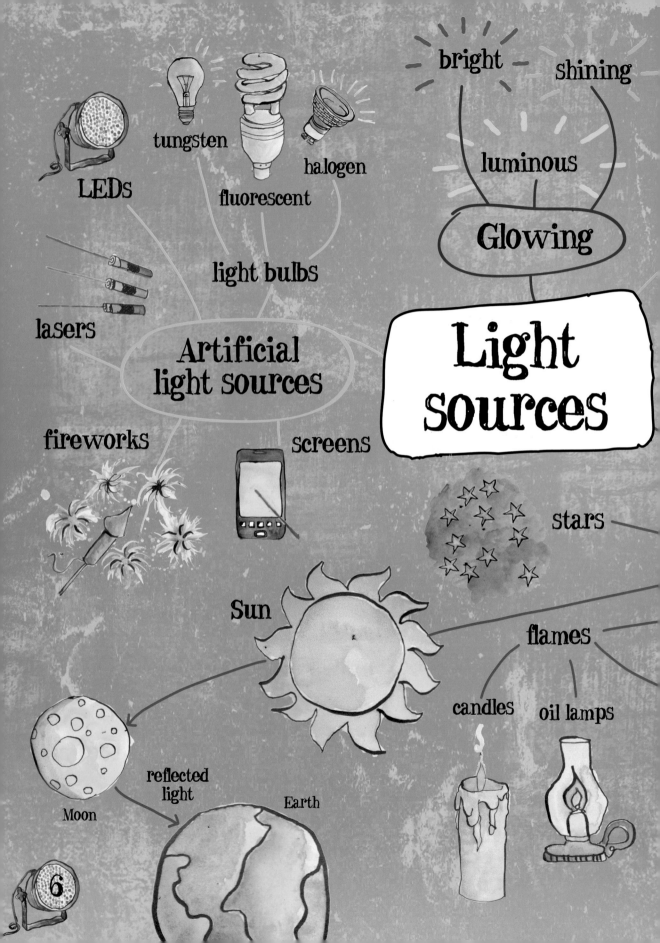

# Light sources

**Glowing**
- bright
- shining
- luminous

**Artificial light sources**
- LEDs
- tungsten
- fluorescent
- halogen
- light bulbs
- lasers
- fireworks
- screens

Sun

stars

flames
- candles
- oil lamps

Moon — reflected light — Earth

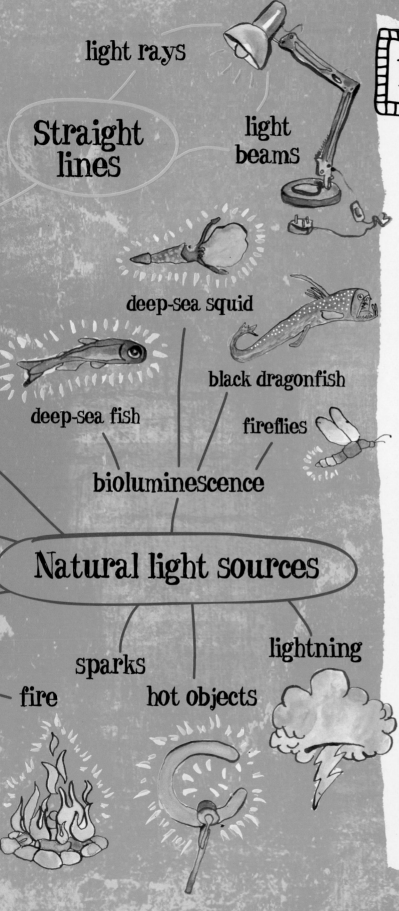

light rays

**Straight lines**

light beams

deep-sea squid

black dragonfish

deep-sea fish

fireflies

**bioluminescence**

**Natural light sources**

sparks

lightning

fire

hot objects

# Light sources

Light comes from many different places or objects, known as light sources. A light source shines or glows as it gives out light energy.

Light sources can be natural, like the Sun, the stars or lightning. Some animals glow with their own light too. Light from living things is called bioluminescence.

We have also invented many artificial light sources, like light bulbs, LEDs and lasers.

### Shadows

Light from a light source travels in straight lines or rays. This means that if something blocks its way, the light cannot go around it. Instead, the object casts a shadow where the light does not reach.

### Reflected light

Some things seem to give out light, but are not light sources. Instead, they are just reflecting light from another source. For example, the Moon seems to glow at night, but it is not a light source. It is reflecting light from the Sun. It does not give out any light of its own.

speed of light is known as 'c'

plants use light energy

light energy powers solar panels

## Energy waves

# Light waves

## Speed of light

in a vacuum: 299,792,458 metres per second
= 670,616,629 miles per hour
= 1,079,252,850 km per hour

in air: 298,925,574 metres per second

in water: 225,407,863 metres per second

in glass: about 200,000,000 metres per second

## Electromagnetic spectrum

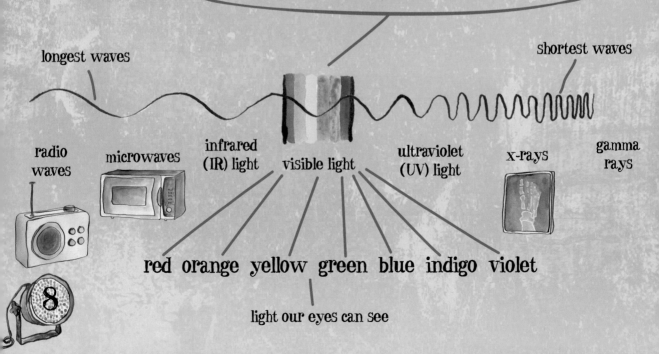

longest waves

shortest waves

radio waves

microwaves

infrared (IR) light

visible light

ultraviolet (UV) light

x-rays

gamma rays

red orange yellow green blue indigo violet

light our eyes can see

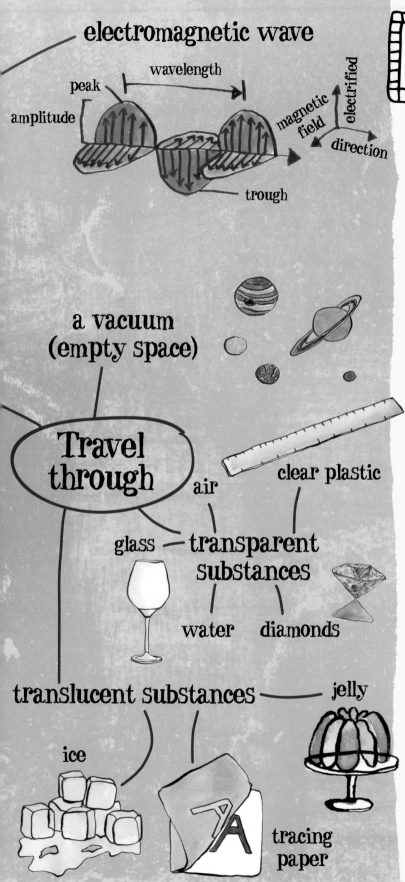

electromagnetic wave

wavelength

peak

amplitude

magnetic field

electrified

direction

trough

a vacuum
(empty space)

Travel
through

air

clear plastic

glass — transparent
substances

water     diamonds

translucent substances — jelly

ice

tracing
paper

Light is a form of energy, but it's hard to understand what it actually is. One way scientists describe light is as a wave. In many ways, light does behave like other waves, such as waves on the surface of water. Light is different, though, because it does not need a substance, such as water, to 'ripple'. Light waves are electromagnetic waves – ripples in the electric and magnetic fields found everywhere. They can travel through a vacuum, and through some materials.

## Big and small

Scientists measure electromagnetic waves according to their length and height. You can't see the waves when you look at a light source – light travels too fast and the measurements are too tiny. The amplitude is the height of the wave. This decides how bright the light is. The wavelength is the length from one wave to the next. This decides what type or colour of light the light wave is.

cat's eyes at night

fish scales

shiny beetles

**In nature**

shiny berries

periscope

angle of incidence

angle of reflection

I    R

incoming ray

reflected ray

**angles**

**Angles of incidence**

# Reflection

night safety gear

**Useful reflections**

safety mirror

wing mirror

rearview mirror

cat's eyes

roof tile

**rough or dull**

fabric

rubber

diffuse reflection

stone

# Reflection

Light waves are reflected, or bounce away, when they hit surfaces. Just like a ball bouncing on the ground, a light wave will reflect off a surface in a particular direction, depending on the direction it came from. The angle of incidence is the angle at which a beam of light is reflected from a surface. The angle of reflection is the angle at which a reflected beam of light leaves a surface.

## Smooth surfaces

A smooth, flat, shiny surface acts as a mirror. Light waves reflect off it neatly, in parallel lines. This is called a clear reflection. This is why you can see yourself clearly in a mirror. If a smooth surface is curved or bent, like a spoon, it can reflect a clear, but distorted or stretched image.

## Rough surfaces

Rough, bumpy or dull surfaces reflect light in many directions, making the light waves scatter. This is called a diffuse reflection. Instead of seeing a reflected image, we see the textured surface.

spoon

reflect a distorted image

raindrop

ball bearings

convex surface

concave surface

curved mirror

Smooth and curved

## Types of surface

flat/smooth/shiny

mirror

clear reflection

still pond

lots of mirrors

kaleidoscope

glitterball

11

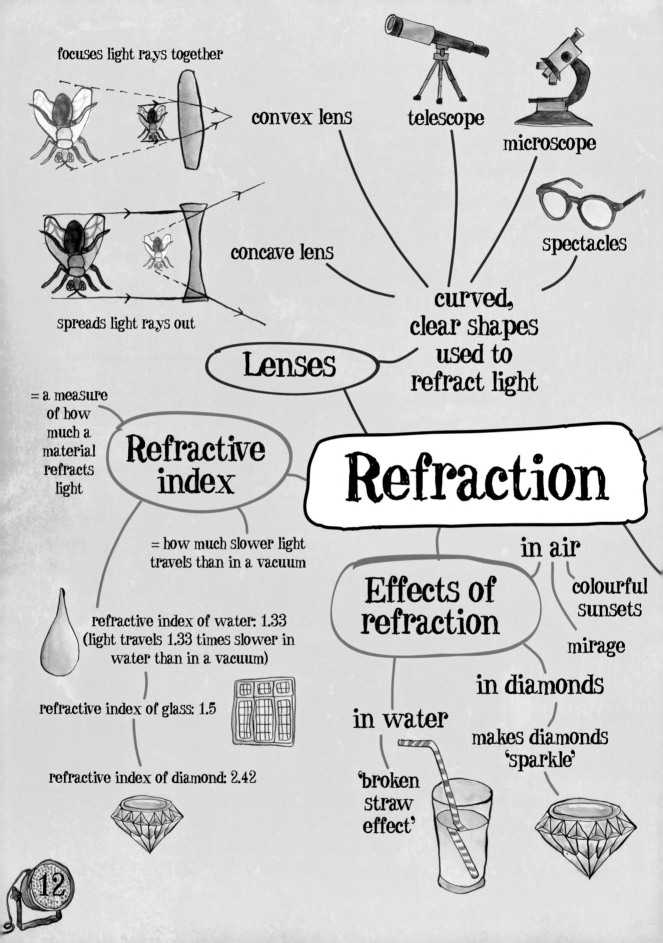

focuses light rays together

convex lens

telescope

microscope

concave lens

spectacles

spreads light rays out

curved, clear shapes used to refract light

Lenses

= a measure of how much a material refracts light

Refractive index

Refraction

= how much slower light travels than in a vacuum

in air

colourful sunsets

Effects of refraction

mirage

refractive index of water: 1.33 (light travels 1.33 times slower in water than in a vacuum)

in diamonds

in water

refractive index of glass: 1.5

makes diamonds 'sparkle'

'broken straw effect'

refractive index of diamond: 2.42

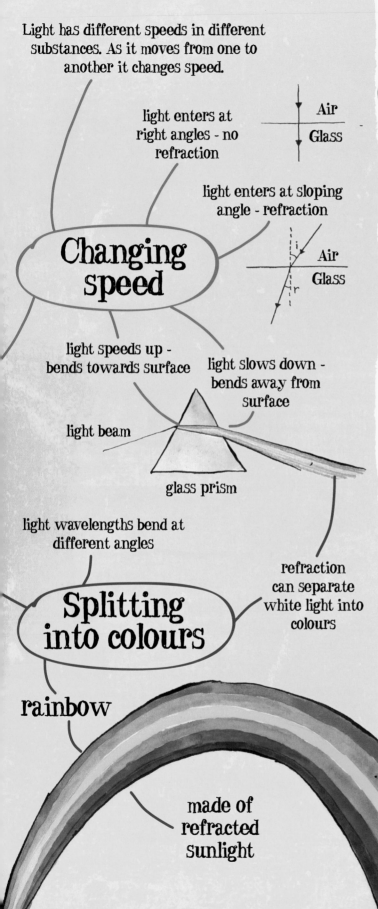

Light has different speeds in different substances. As it moves from one to another it changes speed.

light enters at right angles - no refraction

Air

Glass

light enters at sloping angle - refraction

i

Air

Glass

r

## Changing speed

light speeds up - bends towards surface

light slows down - bends away from surface

light beam

glass prism

light wavelengths bend at different angles

## Splitting into colours

refraction can separate white light into colours

rainbow

made of refracted sunlight

Light can pass through one substance, like air, and into another, like glass or water. When this happens, the light changes speed, and this can make it bend and change direction. This bending is called refraction.

### Lines and angles
If a light beam enters a substance at right-angles to the surface, it will change speed, but not bend or refract. It only refracts if it enters the new substance at a sloping angle (see 'broken straw effect').

### Splitting into colours
White light, such as daylight or the light from a lamp, is made up of all the colours of light mixed together. The different colours have different wavelengths. When a beam of white light is refracted, the different wavelengths bend at slightly different angles. This makes them start to separate from each other. Sometimes you can see this as a band of rainbow colours (see 'glass prism').

# Seeing

We see because our eyes can detect light. We see light from glowing light sources, and also the light that is reflected off objects. So when you switch on the light in a room, you don't just see the glowing light bulb – you also see all the objects in the room, because the light from the bulb bounces off them.

## Eyeballs

Humans have two eyes. Each one is a rubbery ball, or eyeball, full of a clear jelly called vitreous humour. At the front of the eyeball there is a hole, or pupil, to let light in, and a lens to refract the light and direct it to the back of the eye.

At the back of the eye is the retina, a layer of light-detecting cells. They are linked to the brain, and send messages to it about the patterns of light you can see. The brain makes sense of the patterns it receives, so you can work out what you are looking at.

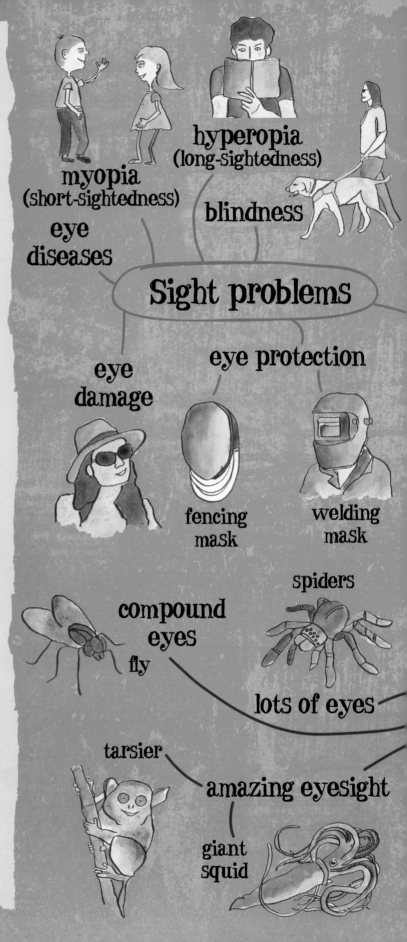

myopia
(short-sightedness)

hyperopia
(long-sightedness)

blindness

eye
diseases

Sight problems

eye protection

eye
damage

fencing
mask

welding
mask

spiders

compound
eyes
fly

lots of eyes

tarsier

amazing eyesight

giant
squid

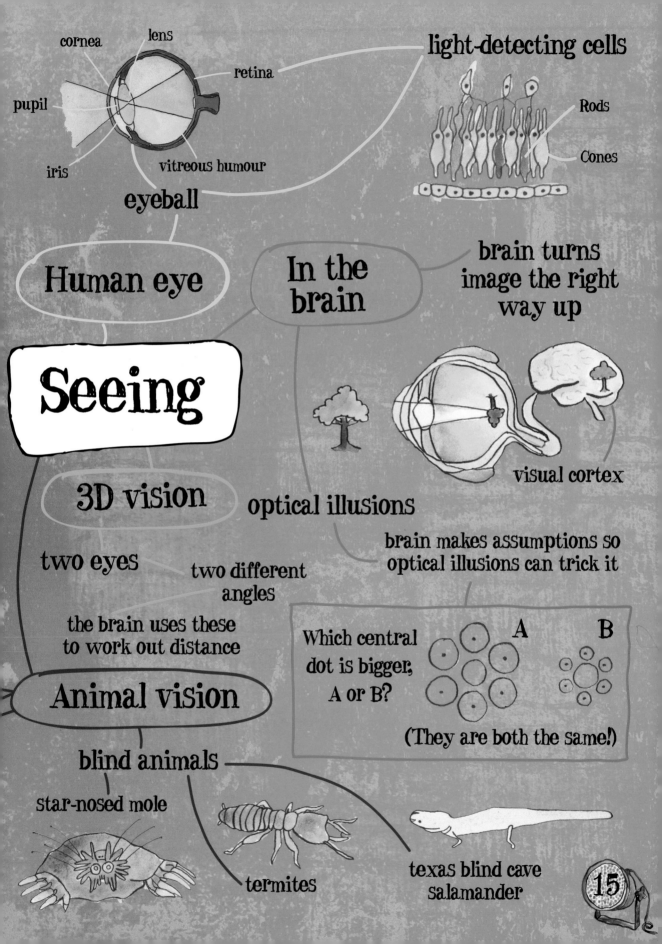

cornea

lens

retina

pupil

iris

vitreous humour

eyeball

light-detecting cells

Rods

Cones

Human eye

In the brain

brain turns image the right way up

Seeing

visual cortex

3D vision

optical illusions

two eyes

two different angles

the brain uses these to work out distance

Animal vision

blind animals

star-nosed mole

termites

texas blind cave salamander

brain makes assumptions so optical illusions can trick it

Which central dot is bigger, A or B?

A

B

(They are both the same!)

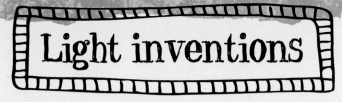

# Light inventions

Light is a huge part of our lives, and we've been inventing new ways to use it for centuries. Early inventions included shadow clocks and sundials, which used the Sun's shadow to tell the time.

## Light in the night

Making our own light sources has always been important, as it means we can see and do things at night, when the Sun is down. Artificial light sources range from early oil lamps to modern electric light bulbs and LEDS.

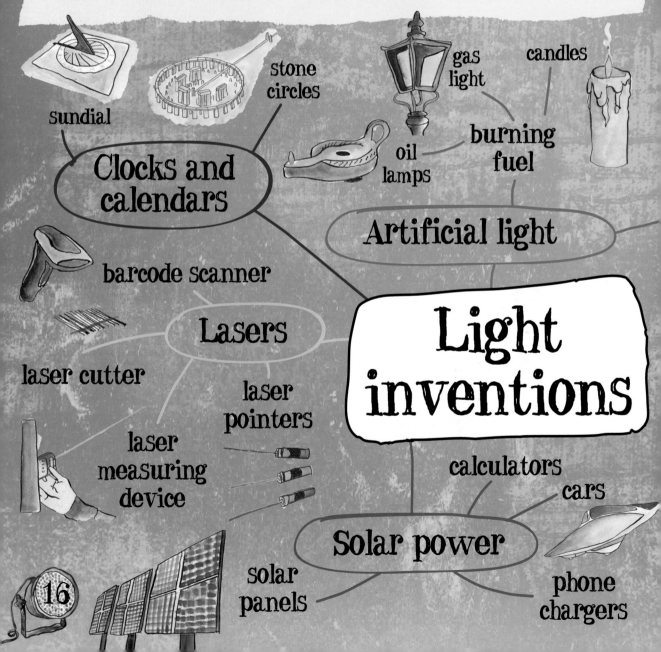

sundial

stone circles

gas light

candles

oil lamps

burning fuel

**Clocks and calendars**

**Artificial light**

barcode scanner

**Lasers**

laser cutter

laser pointers

laser measuring device

# Light inventions

calculators

cars

**Solar power**

solar panels

phone chargers

## Recording light

Cameras date back to around the year 1000, when the scientist Alhazen developed the camera obscura, which could capture an image inside a room. Since then, we have worked out how to record light patterns, creating photography, film and TV.

## Light signals

Light is also a form of communication. In ancient times people could send a message a long way by lighting a string of bonfires. Now, information travels at the speed of light along fibre-optic cables.

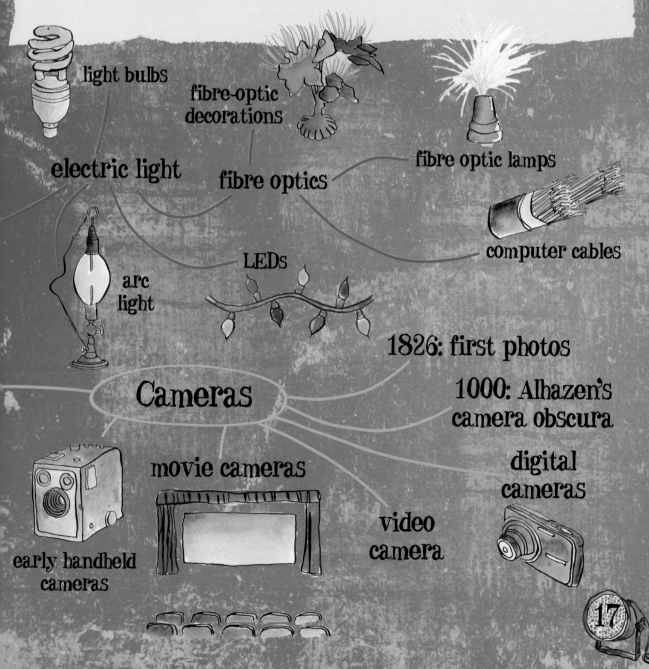

light bulbs

fibre-optic decorations

fibre optic lamps

electric light

fibre optics

computer cables

arc light

LEDs

1826: first photos

Cameras

1000: Alhazen's camera obscura

movie cameras

digital cameras

video camera

early handheld cameras

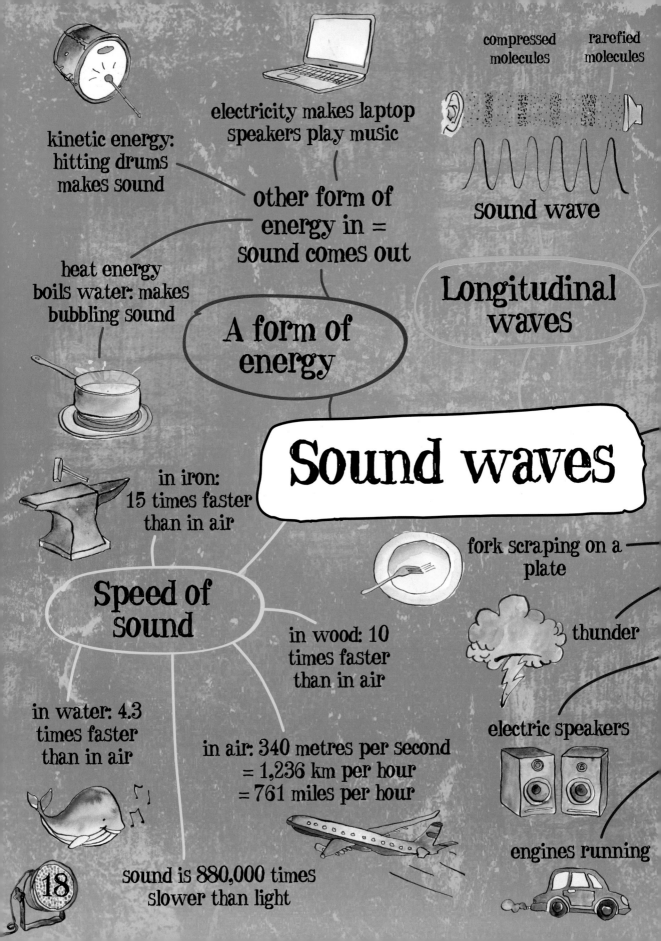

kinetic energy: hitting drums makes sound

electricity makes laptop speakers play music

compressed molecules

rarefied molecules

sound wave

other form of energy in = sound comes out

heat energy boils water: makes bubbling sound

A form of energy

Longitudinal waves

# Sound waves

in iron: 15 times faster than in air

fork scraping on a plate

thunder

Speed of sound

in wood: 10 times faster than in air

in water: 4.3 times faster than in air

electric speakers

in air: 340 metres per second
= 1,236 km per hour
= 761 miles per hour

engines running

sound is 880,000 times slower than light

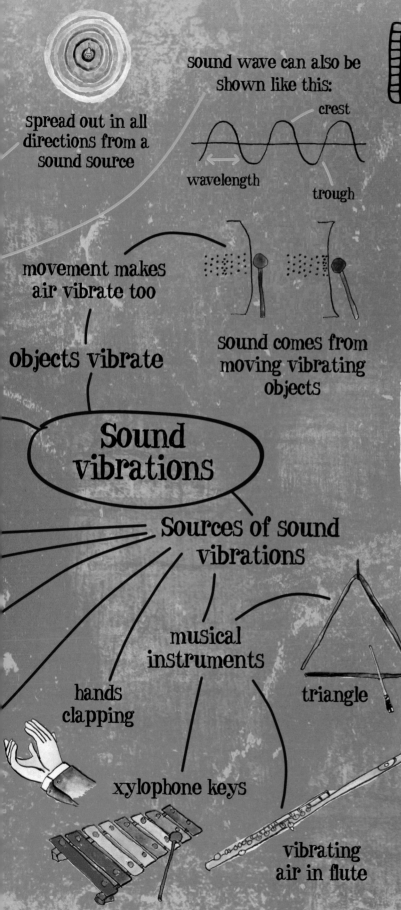

spread out in all directions from a sound source

sound wave can also be shown like this:

crest

wavelength

trough

movement makes air vibrate too

objects vibrate

sound comes from moving vibrating objects

## Sound vibrations

Sources of sound vibrations

musical instruments

hands clapping

triangle

xylophone keys

vibrating air in flute

# Sound waves

Like light, sound is a form of energy that travels in waves. However, sound waves are not like light waves or ocean waves. Instead of rippling up and down or side to side, they make matter move back and forth as they travel through it. This type of wave is called a longitudinal wave.

**Sound waves**
Sound is made by objects moving or vibrating (shaking to and fro very fast). As the object moves, it pushes the air around it. This makes the molecules (tiny particles) in the air push against the molecules next to them, and the movement spreads out in all directions.

**Sound in a substance**
Unlike light, sound cannot travel through an empty vacuum. Sound waves can travel only if they have a substance, or medium, to travel through, such as air, water, or the human body.

# Volume

When you listen to music or watch TV, you might turn the volume up or down. Volume is the loudness of a sound. It depends on the amplitude of the sound wave – how much it makes molecules move to and fro, and how much energy it carries.

We use units called decibels, or dB, to measure and describe sound volume. The decibel scale has no upper limit, but most sounds fall somewhere between zero and 200 dB.

Big volcanic eruption – 150 dB
Jet plane taking off – 135 dB
Thunderstorm – 115 dB
Loud rock concert – 100 dB
Busy road – 70 dB
Busy classroom – 60 dB
Normal speech – 50 dB
Leaves waving in a breeze – 30 dB
Quietest sound you can hear – 0 dB

Decibels actually measure sound pressure – how much a sound makes the air push or press on things around it. There is a huge range of sound pressure, from the quietest sounds like a leaf falling, to the loudest like a volcano exploding. Because of this, the decibel scale is unusual. Each 10db you go up the scale doesn't add 10 units – it multiplies by 10 units. So 30 dB is ten times louder than 20 dB, and 40 dB is ten times louder than 30 dB. This is called a logarithmic scale.

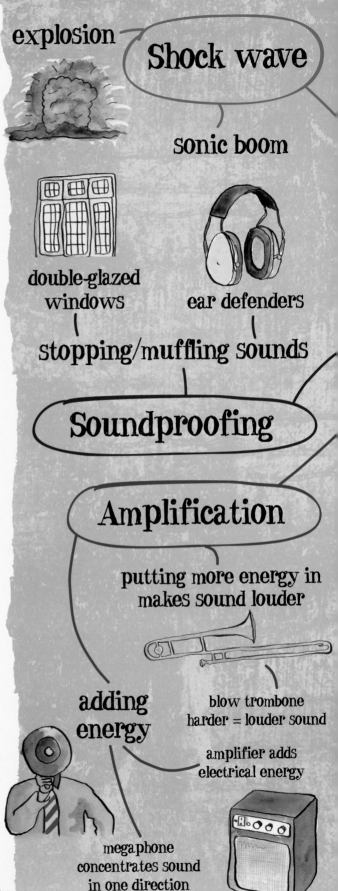

explosion

## Shock wave

sonic boom

double-glazed windows

ear defenders

stopping/muffling sounds

## Soundproofing

## Amplification

putting more energy in makes sound louder

adding energy

blow trombone harder = louder sound

amplifier adds electrical energy

megaphone concentrates sound in one direction

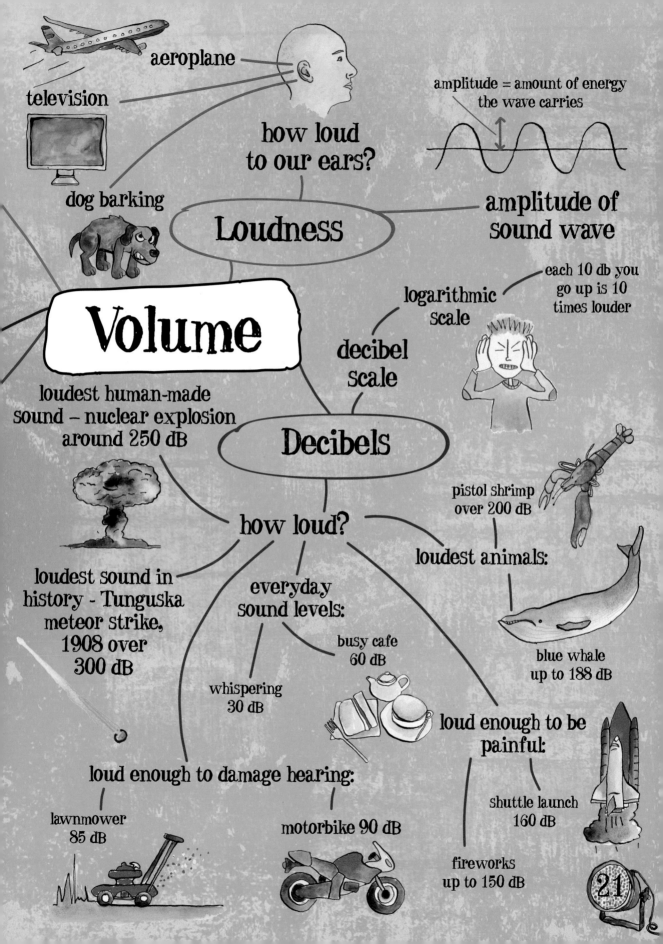

aeroplane

television

dog barking

how loud to our ears?

amplitude = amount of energy the wave carries

Loudness

amplitude of sound wave

**Volume**

logarithmic scale

each 10 db you go up is 10 times louder

decibel scale

loudest human-made sound – nuclear explosion around 250 dB

Decibels

pistol shrimp over 200 dB

loudest animals:

how loud?

loudest sound in history - Tunguska meteor strike, 1908 over 300 dB

everyday sound levels:

busy cafe 60 dB

blue whale up to 188 dB

whispering 30 dB

loud enough to be painful:

loud enough to damage hearing:

shuttle launch 160 dB

lawnmower 85 dB

motorbike 90 dB

fireworks up to 150 dB

21

# Pitch

Pitch means how high or low a sound is. Tinkling cutlery, a phone ringing and children's voices are high-pitched sounds. A tiger's roar and a bus engine are low-pitched sounds.

**Frequency**

The pitch of a sound is decided by its frequency – the number of sound waves it gives out per second, also known as 'cycles per second'. We use a unit called Hertz or Hz to measure frequency. For example, the middle C key on a piano has a string that vibrates 261 times per second. It makes a sound that has a frequency of 261 Hz.

The faster something vibrates to and fro, the higher the frequency of the sound waves, and the higher the pitch we hear. Small things tend to vibrate faster than large things. This is why a small bell makes a high-pitched noise and a big bell makes a low-pitched noise.

## How many Hertz?

| | |
|---|---|
| birdsong | 1,000-5,000 Hz |
| child's voice | 300-400 Hz |
| woman's voice | around 210 Hz |
| man's voice | around 125 Hz |
| dog growling | 60-90 Hz |
| blue whale song | 25 Hz |

vocal cords vibrate in throat

talking
(pitch changes to change meanings)

## Speaking voice

singing - voice makes notes

Yeah. YEAH! Yeah?

**Frequency**

speed of vibration

Hertz ( Hz) =
number of sound
waves or 'cycles'
per second

**Pitch**

'perfect
pitch'

**Music**

scale
(series of
notes used to
make music)

notes
(sound with a
particular pitch)

melody
(pattern of notes)

harmony
(different notes
played together)

### What changes pitch?

Lower pitch

bigger
objects

longer
strings

looser
strings

longer
tubes

Higher pitch

smaller
objects

shorter
strings

tighter
strings

shorter
tubes

musical
instruments
(change pitch to play
different notes)

piano
(different keys
and strings)

violin
(press on strings to
make them shorter)

trombone
(move slide to make tube
longer and shorter)

23

# Echoes

Like light, sound can bounce or reflect off a surface. Reflected sound is called an echo. For example, you might hear your voice echoing back to you if you shout opposite a large cliff or wall. As sound travels much more slowly than light, it can take a second or so for the echo to come back.

## Echoes everywhere

If echoes are all jumbled up together, as in most rooms, they are known as reverberation. A clear, separate echo happens only when there is enough time for the sound to travel away and then bounce back without overlapping itself.

Sounds reflects better off hard, flat surfaces. Soft or rough surfaces absorb sounds. This is why an empty room sounds more 'echoey' than a room full of furniture, carpets and curtains.

## Useful echoes

By measuring the time it takes an echo to come back, we can measure distances. We use this to make images of the seabed, the shape of a room or even our insides.

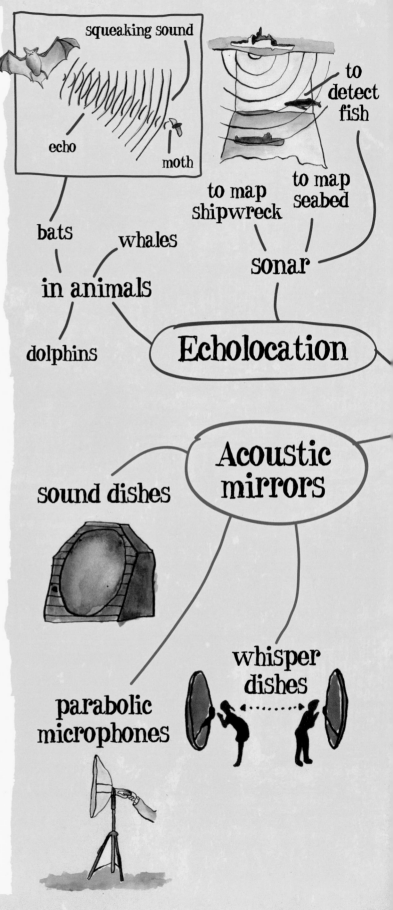

squeaking sound

echo

moth

to detect fish

bats

whales

to map shipwreck

to map seabed

in animals

sonar

dolphins

Echolocation

Acoustic mirrors

sound dishes

whisper dishes

parabolic microphones

sound source    surface

outgoing sound →

← reflected sound

wine glass    stone

brick

echoey surfaces

non-echoey surfaces

**Reflected sound**

# Echoes

curtains    trees    rubber

**Famous echoes**

Whispering Gallery, St Paul's Cathedral, London

**Reverberation**

overlapping, jumbled echoes

sound box
(hollow, open part of a musical instrument)

empty rooms

Echo Wall, Temple of Heaven, Beijing, China

guiro    guitar

caves    concert halls

sound reverberates inside

25

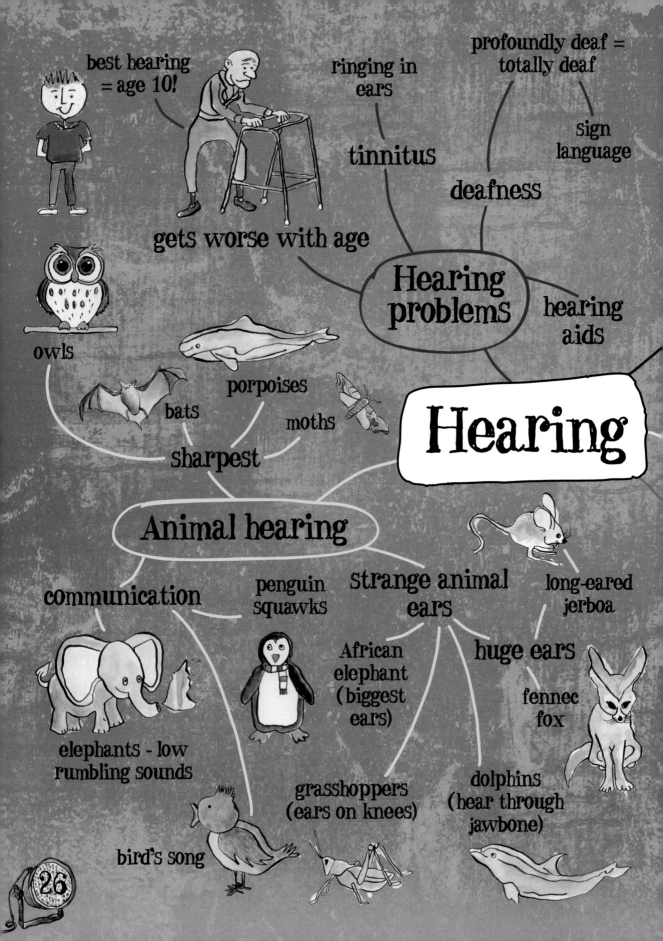

# Hearing

**Hearing problems**
- best hearing = age 10!
- gets worse with age
- ringing in ears
- tinnitus
- deafness
  - profoundly deaf = totally deaf
  - sign language
- hearing aids

**Animal hearing**
- sharpest
  - owls
  - bats
  - porpoises
  - moths
- communication
  - elephants - low rumbling sounds
  - penguin squawks
  - bird's song
- strange animal ears
  - African elephant (biggest ears)
  - grasshoppers (ears on knees)
  - dolphins (hear through jawbone)
  - huge ears
    - long-eared jerboa
    - fennec fox

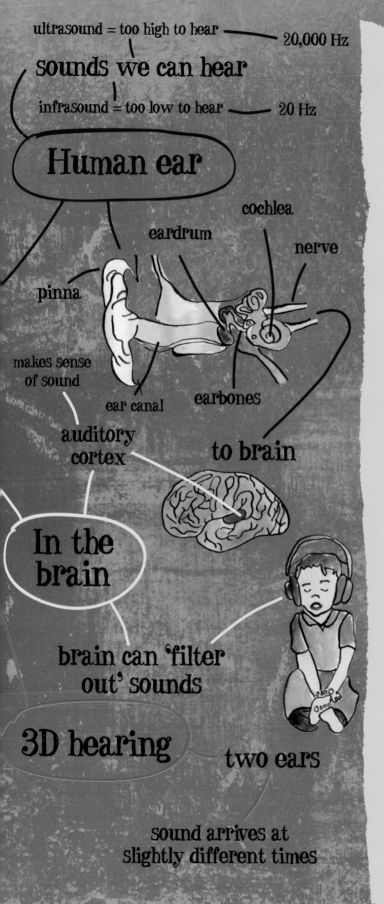

ultrasound = too high to hear —— 20,000 Hz

sounds we can hear

infrasound = too low to hear —— 20 Hz

## Human ear

cochlea

eardrum

nerve

pinna

makes sense of sound

ear canal

earbones

auditory cortex

to brain

## In the brain

brain can 'filter out' sounds

## 3D hearing

two ears

sound arrives at slightly different times

We hear sounds when sound waves spread out from the object that made them, and reach our ears. Inside each of our ears is a small, tightly stretched disc of skin called the eardrum. It is called this because it's very like the skin of a drum.

### Eardrum
As sound waves hit the eardrum, they make it vibrate at the same frequency as the sound itself. The vibrations are passed on inside the ear, through a series of tiny bones, and into the snail-shaped cochlea. From here, the vibrations are turned into nerve signals and sent into the brain.

### Making sense of sound
Your eardrum can sense only vibrations. All the different, amazingly complicated things you can hear – like people talking, music or traffic noise – are made up of patterns of vibrations of different amplitudes (strengths) and frequencies. Two or more sounds at once just make a more complex pattern of vibrations.

# Sound inventions

In 1876, American inventor Thomas Edison made a huge breakthrough. He managed to record his own voice, then play it back, using a machine he called the phonograph. No one had ever done this before. Today, over 130 years later, we're surrounded by recorded sound, and machines that play sounds to us.

## Making new sounds

We've had musical instruments for thousands of years, but since computers were invented, we've

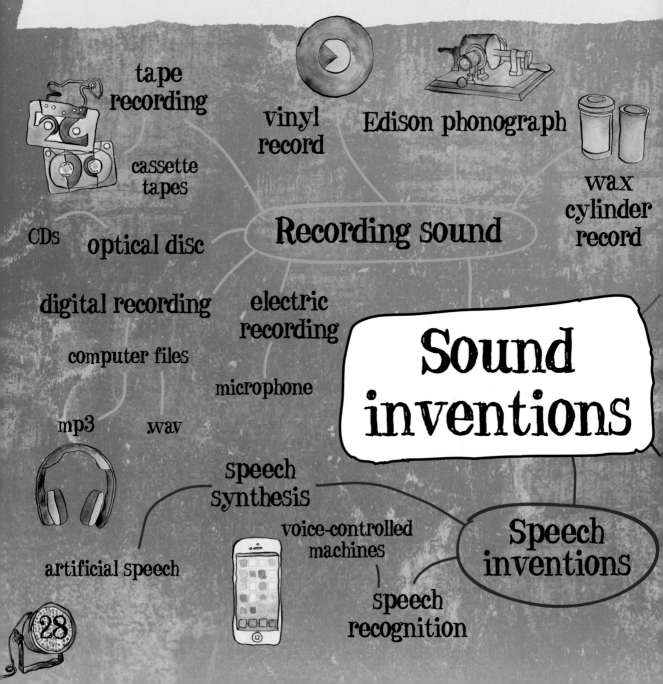

tape recording

cassette tapes

vinyl record

Edison phonograph

wax cylinder record

CDs    optical disc

Recording sound

digital recording

electric recording

computer files

microphone

mp3    .wav

speech synthesis

## Sound inventions

voice-controlled machines

artificial speech

Speech inventions

speech recognition

also been able to create new, electronic music and other sounds. You can hear them in many pop songs, in film special effects and from all the machines around you that go 'beep', like hi-fis, phones and washing machines.

**Sound as a tool**
Sound isn't just something we listen to. There are all kinds of inventions that use sounds – especially ultrasound and infrasound – to do useful jobs, like scanning inside the body, killing germs or forecasting earthquakes.

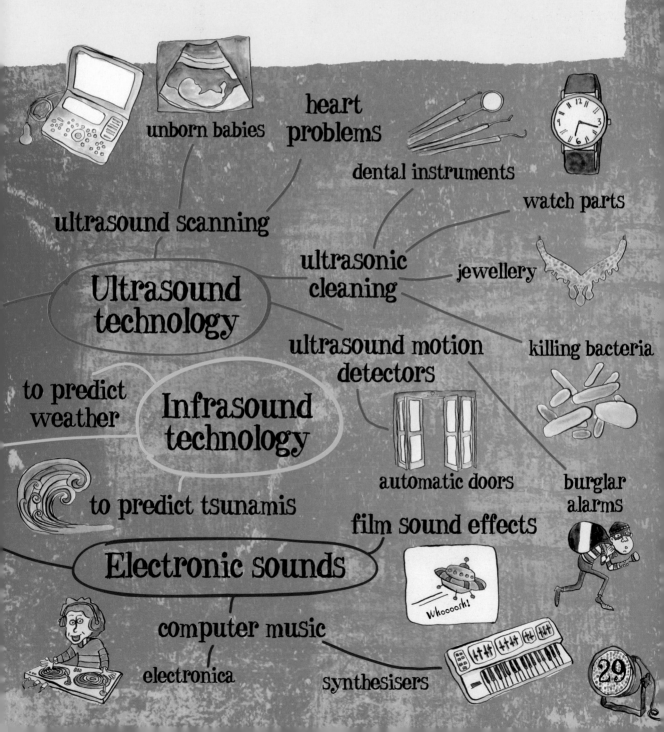

unborn babies

heart problems

dental instruments

watch parts

ultrasound scanning

ultrasonic cleaning

jewellery

**Ultrasound technology**

ultrasound motion detectors

killing bacteria

to predict weather

**Infrasound technology**

automatic doors

burglar alarms

to predict tsunamis

film sound effects

**Electronic sounds**

Whoooosh!

computer music

electronica

synthesisers

29

# Glossary

**amplitude** The strength of a wave.

**bioluminescence** Light given off by living things.

**camera obscura** Type of early camera that captured an image inside a room.

**cochlea** Snail-shaped part inside the ear.

**compressed** Squeezed together, used to describe molecules in a sound wave.

**cornea** Clear covering over the front of the eye.

**crest** The peak or highest point of a wave.

**decibels (dB)** Units used to measure the power or loudness of sound.

**ear canal** Tube leading from the outside to the inside of the ear.

**eardrum** Thin, tightly stretched skin inside the ear that picks up vibrations.

**echo** Sound that has reflected off a surface and returned to its source.

**echolocation** Way of sensing objects from the sound echoes that bounce off them.

**electromagnetic waves** Waves or ripples in electric and magnetic fields.

**electromagnetic spectrum** Range of electromagnetic waves of different wavelengths.

**energy** The power to do work or make things happen.

**energy waves** Waves that carry some types of energy, such as sound and light.

**frequency (of sound)** Number of sound waves or vibrations in a second.

**Hertz (Hz)** Unit used to measure sound frequency.

**iris** The coloured, ring-shaped part of the eye.

**laser** Device that gives out a narrow beam of light.

**LEDs** Light-Emitting Diodes, a type of electronic light source.

**lens** A curved, clear shape for refracting and directing light.

**logarithmic scale** Scale in which going up by 10 points means multiplying by 10.

**longitudinal wave** Energy wave that makes the substance it travels through move back and forth, not side to side or up and down.

**medium** Substance that sound travels through.

**molecules** Tiny units that substances are made up of.

**optical fibre** Thin, flexible glass fibre that can carry light waves along inside it.

**parallel** Lying side by side and never meeting.

**phonograph** The first sound recording device, built by Thomas Edison.

**pitch** How high or low a sound is, decided by its f**requenc**y.

**prism** A clear 3D shape with flat surfaces at angles to each other, for refracting light.

**pupil** The hole in the middle of the front of the eye, which appears as a black dot.

**rarefied** Spaced widely apart, used to describe molecules in a sound wave.

**rays** Beams or 'lines' of light travelling out from a light source.

**reflection** Light bouncing off a surface.

**refraction** Changing direction when passing from one clear substance into another.

**retina** Layer at the back of the eyeball that senses light.

**reverberation** Jumble of echoes that are not clearly separated from each other.

**shadow** Dark area created where light rays cannot pass through an object.

**technology** Inventions, tools and machines designed to solve problems and do tasks.

**trough** The lowest point of a wave.

**vitreous humour** Clear, jelly-like substance inside the eyeball.

**volume** The loudness or strength of a sound.

**wave** Vibration or rippling that carries a form of energy from one place to another.

**wavelength** The length from one point on a wave, to the same point on the next wave.

# Index